For Sally, Milt, and Ad, who filled my childhood with happy sounds
—W.P.

For Jill, with thanks
—H.K.

With special thanks to Dr. John M. Sooy at Rowan University for his expert advice.

The illustrations in this book were created with pen and ink, watercolors, and pastels on Rives BFK paper.

The *Let's-Read-and-Find-Out Science* book series was originated by Dr. Franklyn M. Branley, Astronomer Emeritus and former Chairman of the American Museum–Hayden Planetarium, and was formerly co-edited by him and Dr. Roma Gans, Professor Emeritus of Childhood Education, Teachers College, Columbia University. Text and illustrations for each of the books in the series are checked for accuracy by an expert in the relevant field. For more information about Let's-Read-and-Find-Out Science books, write to HarperCollins Children's Books, 10 East 53rd Street, New York, NY 10022, or visit our web site at http://www.harperchildrens.com.

Library of Congress Cataloging-in-Publication Data
Pfeffer, Wendy, date
 Sounds all around / by Wendy Pfeffer ; illustrated by Holly Keller.
  p.   cm. — (Let's-read-and-find-out science. Stage I)
 Summary: Explains how sounds are made and the purposes they serve for both humans and other animals.
 ISBN 0-06-027711-4. — ISBN 0-06-027712-2 (lib. bdg.) — ISBN 0-06-445177-1 (pbk.)
 1. Sound—Juvenile literature.   [1. Sound.]   I. Keller, Holly, ill.   II. Title.   III. Series.
QC225.5P49   1999   97-17993
534—dc21   CIP
                                                                                      AC

Typography by Elynn Cohen and Christine Casarsa
1   2   3   4   5   6   7   8   9   10
❖
First Edition

BUZZZ

Snap your fingers. Clap your hands. Whistle!
Clatter some pans. You're making sounds!

4

Crinkle-crunch through dry leaves.

CRUNCH

SPLASH

Splish-splash in a puddle.

Make happy sounds!

Sad sounds!

Scary sounds!

Mad sounds!

HA HA

WAAH

BOO

Grrrrr

Shake a can of marbles . . . rattle, rattle, rattle.
Shake a can of cheese puffs . . . pluff, pluff, pluff.
Shake a can of pencils . . . clank, clank, clank.
 Your sounds fill the air.

PLUFF
PLUFF

CHEESE
FFS

CLANK
CLANK

Make more sounds. Sing. Talk. Hum. These sounds come out of your mouth, but they start in your throat.

Feel your throat as you sing, talk, or hum.

Your fingertips tingle because your vocal cords shake to make sounds.

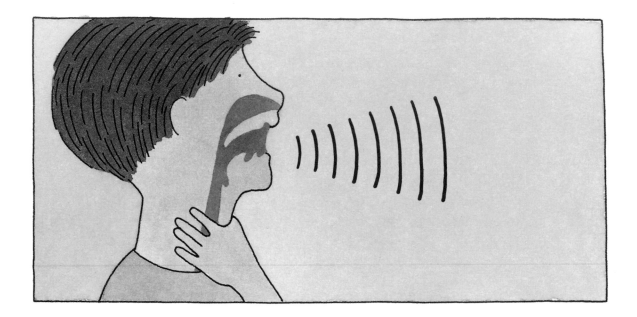

They shake back and forth very fast.

This is called vibrating.

And that makes the air around them vibrate.

These vibrations move through the air in waves called sound waves.

Now, be quiet. Feel your throat. Your vocal cords are still.

They're not vibrating, so there's no sound.

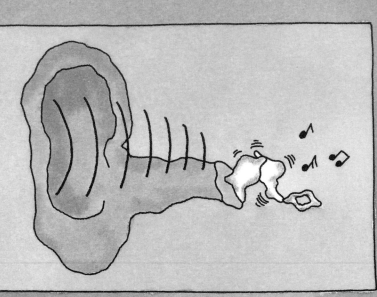

You can't see sound waves,
but when they reach your ear,
tiny bones in your ear vibrate.
Then you hear the sound.

Beating a drum makes it vibrate, and then the air around it vibrates. These vibrations ripple through the air. They travel from the drum to your ears, and you hear the sound of the drum.

Long ago, people used drum sounds to send
messages. They beat high sounds, low sounds,
fast sounds, slow sounds. These sounds traveled
through the air, from village to village. Different
drumbeats sent different messages, such as

Rain clouds are forming or

A new leader has been chosen.

13

People still use sounds to send messages.
Clapping hands says "Good job."

CLAP

KNOCK
KNOCK

A knock on the door
asks "Is anyone home?"

EEEEEEEEEEE

And the siren on a fire truck
means "Get out of the way!"

CLUCK, CLUCK, CLUCK

Animals use sounds to send messages, too. A hen clucks to call her chicks.

A ruffed grouse makes a drumming sound to attract a mate.

THUMP

HOWWWWL !

And a howler monkey roars to keep other howlers out of its territory. A howler's roar is one of the loudest animal sounds in the world. No wonder other howlers stay out of the way.

In the dark, a bat stays out of the way of an object in its flight path by making high squeaking sounds. Its sound waves hit the barn. The sound bounces back. These echoes warn the bat to change direction before it bumps into the barn.

A bat finds food using echoes, too. Sound waves bounce off insects. In total darkness a bat can *locate* 600 insects an hour by listening for the *echoes*. This is called *echolocation*.

Sound waves travel through solid ground as well as air. A snake has no ears. To hear, it puts its head on the ground. A bone in its head feels the sound vibrations. They warn the snake that an enemy, maybe a mongoose, lurks nearby.

Sound waves travel through water, too. A mother whale can find her baby by sending clicking sounds through the water. When the sound waves bump into her calf, echoes bounce back. The mother whale listens. She hears the echoes and knows where her baby is.

21

Whales and dolphins locate objects by sending sounds through the water, then listening for the echoes.

People use a device called *sonar* to send sounds in water. When the echoes bounce back, people know how deep the water is. They also discover where submarines, shipwrecks, and schools of fish are.

Sounds are an important part of our lives.

Some sounds, like music, please us.

Some sounds, like a jackhammer, annoy us.

Some sounds are quiet. Some are loud.

How can you measure sounds?
How much you weigh is measured in pounds.
How tall you stand is measured in inches.
How loud you yell is measured in decibels.

Whisper.  **Talk.** **Yell.**

Whisper.
 Whispering measures only about 20 decibels.
Talk.
 Talking measures about 50 decibels.
Yell.
 Wow! A loud yell measures about 80 decibels.

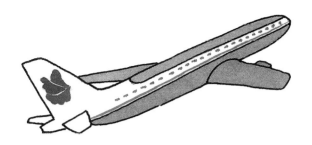

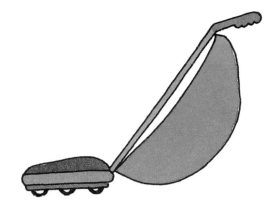

Falling leaves measure only 10 decibels.
A vacuum cleaner 70 decibels.
Loud music 90 decibels.
A jackhammer 100 decibels.
A jet engine 150 decibels.

A space rocket is very loud.
It measures 200 or more decibels.

Some loud sounds can damage your ears. People who are close to airplanes or use jackhammers should protect their ears.

We live in a world of sounds.
Telephones ring. Thunder rumbles.
Water gurgles. Birds chirp.
Bees buzz. Friends talk.
And we laugh, cry, hiccup, sigh.

Sounds are all around. Keep listening!

HERE ARE SOME SOUND ACTIVITIES

MAKE A GUITAR

1. Find an empty tissue box and six different-sized rubber bands.
2. Stretch the rubber bands over the opening in the box.
3. Pluck one rubber band. As it vibrates, listen to the sound.
4. Put your hand on the rubber band. That stops the vibrations and stops the sound.
5. Pluck a different rubber band. It sounds different from the first rubber band because its vibrations are different.
6. Pluck each of the other rubber bands. Listen to the sounds. The thicker the rubber band, the lower the sound will be.
7. Pluck each rubber band and pretend you are playing a guitar.

MAKE MUSICAL GLASSES

1. Ask an adult to help you gather the following:

      eight large water glasses all the same size
      a measuring cup
      a pencil

2. Pour one ounce of water into the first glass, two ounces into the second glass, three ounces into the third glass, and so on until all glasses have been used.
3. Tap each glass with the pencil.
4. Listen to the sound that comes from each glass. The less water in the glass, the lower the sound will be.
5. Tap on each glass. Go up the scale. Go down the scale. Pretend you are playing a tune on a xylophone.

LISTEN TO SOUND TRAVEL THROUGH A SOLID OBJECT

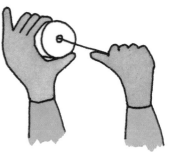

1. With two paper cups and about ten feet of string, make a string telephone.
2. Attach the string to each cup. Here's how:
   - Put a hole in the bottom of each cup.
   - Put the string through each hole.
   - Tie knots in the ends of the string inside each cup to keep the string ends from coming out.
3. Pull the string tight between the cups. The sound stops if the string is loose and cannot vibrate.
4. Ask a friend to whisper into one cup.
5. Put your ear to the other cup and listen. The sound travels through the string, a solid object.
6. Ask your friend to whisper again without using the "telephone."
7. Listen. That sound travels through the air.
8. Which carried your friend's whisper better, the string or the air?

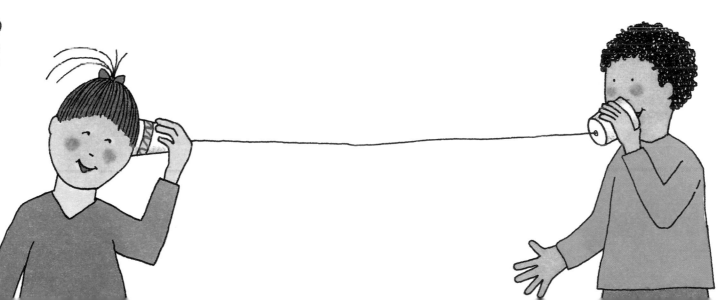

FIND OUT MORE ABOUT SOUND

LISTEN TO SOUNDS AROUND YOU

- Listen in the house. Do you hear a clock ticking, the television blaring, someone laughing? What else do you hear?
- Listen on the front steps. Do you hear a dog barking, a ball bouncing, a horn honking? What else do you hear?
- What could you hear: On a farm? During a storm? In the forest? Near the ocean? By a brook? At the zoo? In the supermarket?

LISTEN TO SOUND TRAVEL THROUGH WATER

- In the bathtub keep your ears above the water. Knock your knuckles underwater on the side of the tub. Can you hear the knocking sound?
- Lie on your back with your ears under the water. Knock underwater again. Can you hear the sound travel through water? Which knocking sounded louder?

SOUNDS MATCHING GAME

- Setting Up:
  1. Collect ten identical containers with lids—such as peanut cans.
  2. With Magic Markers put a red X on five cans. Put a blue X on the other five.
  3. Put an equal amount of marbles into one red can and one blue can. Fill other pairs with paper clips, cotton, pennies, and rice.
  4. Place the red cans together and the blue cans together.
- Game Rules:
  1. The first player shakes a red can, then a blue can. If both cans make the same sound, the player keeps the pair. If not, the cans must be returned.
  2. Take turns. After a match is made, the player should guess what is in each can before opening it.
  3. The player with the most pairs wins. Add other pairs to make the game more challenging.